Susan B. Anthony
FIGHTER for FREEDOM and EQUALITY

by SUZANNE SLADE

illustrated by CRAIG ORBACK

PICTURE WINDOW BOOKS
Minneapolis, Minnesota

Special thanks to our advisers for their expertise:

Sue Gaffney, Volunteer Coordinator, and her volunteers
Susan B. Anthony House
Rochester, New York

Susan Kesselring, M.A., Literacy Educator
Rosemount–Apple Valley–Eagan (Minnesota) School District

Editor: Nick Healy
Designer: Nathan Gassman
Page Production: Melissa Kes
Associate Managing Editor: Christianne Jones
The illustrations in this book were created digitally.
Photo Credit: Bettmann/CORBIS, page 3

Picture Window Books
5115 Excelsior Boulevard, Suite 232
Minneapolis, MN 55416
877-845-8392
www.picturewindowbooks.com

Printed in the United States of America.

Library of Congress Cataloging-in-Publication Data
Slade, Suzanne.
Susan B. Anthony : fighter for freedom and equality / by Suzanne Slade ; illustrated
by Craig Orback.
p. cm. — (Biographies)
Includes bibliographical references and index.
ISBN-13: 978-1-4048-3104-9 (library binding)
ISBN-10: 1-4048-3104-5 (library binding)
1. Anthony, Susan B. (Susan Brownell), 1820-1906—Juvenile literature. 2. Feminists—
United States—Biography—Juvenile literature. 3. Suffragists—United States—
Biography—Juvenile literature. 4. Women social reformers—United States—Biography—
Juvenile literature. 5. Women's rights—United States—History—Juvenile literature.
I. Orback, Craig. II. Title.
HQ1413.A55S54 2006
305.42092—dc22
[B]   2006027226

When Susan B. Anthony was young, white men had more rights than other people. Susan believed everyone should have equal rights. As an adult, she shared her ideas about equality. She gave many speeches. She started a newspaper. She worked to change laws. In doing so, Susan changed the lives of all Americans.

This is the story of
Susan B. Anthony.

Susan was born in Adams, Massachusetts, in 1820. Her parents belonged to the Quaker religion. Quakers believed that everyone was equal. They also thought it was important for children to learn. Susan learned to read when she was just 4 years old. Her grandmother taught Susan and her sisters.

As a child, Susan saw that boys and girls were treated differently. Only boys were allowed to sit in the front rows at school. Also, girls were left out of important lessons. Susan told her father she wanted an equal chance to learn. He turned part of their house into a school. There, all children were treated the same.

Susan began teaching when she was 15. Five years later, she took a teaching job in New York. She was paid $2.50 a week. The teacher who had the job before Susan was a man. He earned $10 a week. Susan thought men and women should get the same pay for the same work.

In 1846, Susan became the head mistress of a school called Canajoharie Academy in New York. Although she enjoyed her job, she kept thinking about how women were treated unfairly. Women were only allowed to do certain jobs, such as teach or work in factories. Husbands got all of the money their wives earned. Women could not vote or own property. They could not even wear pants.

Susan left her job at Canajoharie in 1849. She returned to her parents' home, where she took charge of the family farm. She also started to work on an important issue.

Susan joined the temperance movement. People in this movement believed alcohol caused many problems. For example, they thought men who drank too much alcohol were unkind to women.

In 1851, Susan met Elizabeth Cady Stanton. Elizabeth was a writer, and she had strong ideas about helping women. Susan and Elizabeth became good friends. They worked together to teach others about equality. Susan began to travel around the country, speaking and marching in protests. Elizabeth wrote many of Susan's speeches.

The Civil War began in 1861. As the United States fought over slavery, Susan spoke out about why all people should be free. She helped get 400,000 people to sign a petition against slavery. This petition showed support for the 13th Amendment to the U.S. Constitution. The amendment freed all slaves. It was approved by the states after the Civil War ended in 1865.

After the Civil War, Susan returned to her battle for women's rights. She fought with her words, giving about 200 speeches each year. Susan traveled around the country in wagons and trains. She spoke in barns, schools, and cabins. Her travels were difficult, with little time for rest. Still, Susan kept speaking.

In 1868, Susan and Elizabeth Cady Stanton started a newspaper. They called it *The Revolution*. The paper shared many of Susan's ideas, including the idea that women and men should get equal pay for equal work. Susan also pushed to win women the right to vote.

Due to Susan's bravery and hard work, many people slowly began to change their minds about how women should be treated. Susan fought for women's rights until she died in 1906.

The Life of Susan B. Anthony

1820	Born on February 15 in Adams, Massachusetts
1846	Became the head mistress of Canajoharie Academy and earned $110 per year
1849	Left Canajoharie Academy and returned home
1851	Met Elizabeth Cady Stanton
1865	Helped to pass the 13th Amendment, which freed all slaves
1868	With Elizabeth Cady Stanton, started a newspaper called *The Revolution*
1872	Arrested for voting in Rochester, New York
1906	Died at her home in Rochester on March 13 at age 86

Did You Know?

- Susan came from a large family. She had four sisters and two brothers.

- Even though women were not allowed to vote, Susan went to a voting place in New York in 1872. She was arrested and fined $100. Susan never paid that fine.

- During her 86th birthday party in Washington D.C., Susan gave a famous speech during which she said, "Failure is impossible."

- One of Susan's dreams came true after her death. In 1920, the 19th Amendment was added to the Constitution and women were given the right to vote. People call it the "Susan B. Anthony Amendment."

- Susan was the first woman to appear on a U.S. coin. Silver dollar coins showing Susan's face were made in 1979, 1980, 1981, and 1999. These coins honored Susan and her work for women's rights.

Glossary

alcohol — a drink that can cause people to behave differently

amendment — an addition or correction

Civil War (1861–1865) — the battle between states in the North and the South that led to the end of slavery in the United States

Constitution — the written ideas and laws upon which the U.S. government is based

equality — when things are exactly the same

mistress — a woman in charge of something

petition — a paper that people sign to ask leaders to change a law

Quaker — a person who belongs to a Christian religion that believes all people should have the same rights

slave — a person who is owned by another person

temperance movement — an effort to reduce the use of alcohol and its negative effects

To Learn More

At the Library

Klingel, Cynthia, and Robert B. Noyed. *Susan B. Anthony*. Chanhassen, Minn.: The Child's World, 2003.

McLeese, Don. *Susan B. Anthony*. Vero Beach, Fla.: Rourke Publishing, 2003.

Raatma, Lucia. *Susan B. Anthony*. Minneapolis: Compass Point Books, 2001.

Weidt, Maryann N. *Fighting for Equal Rights*. Minneapolis: Carolrhoda Books, 2004.

On the Web

FactHound offers a safe, fun way to find Web sites related to this book. All of the sites on FactHound have been researched by our staff.

1.   Visit *www.facthound.com*

2.   Type in this special code: 1404831045

3.   Click on the FETCH IT button.

Your trusty FactHound will fetch the best sites for you!

24

Index

Look for all of the books in the Biographies series:

Abraham Lincoln: Lawyer, President, Emancipator

Benjamin Franklin: Writer, Inventor, Statesman

Frederick Douglass: Writer, Speaker, and Opponent of Slavery

George Washington: Farmer, Soldier, President

Harriet Tubman: Hero of the Underground Railroad

Martin Luther King Jr.: Preacher, Freedom Fighter, Peacemaker

Pocahontas: Peacemaker and Friend to the Colonists

Sally Ride: Astronaut, Scientist, Teacher

Susan B. Anthony: Fighter for Freedom and Equality

Thomas Edison: Inventor, Scientist, and Genius